Helium Resources of the United States–2003

Technical Note 415

June 2004

By B.D.Gage
Petroleum Engineer
Bureau of Land Management
Amarillo Field Office
Amarillo, Texas

D.L. Driskill
Geologist
Bureau of Land Management
Amarillo Field Office
Amarillo, Texas

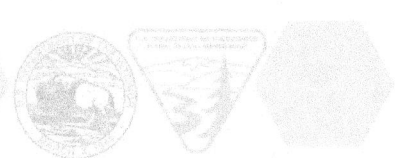

United States Department of the Interior
Bureau of Land Management

Unit of Measure Abbreviations
Used in Report

Bcf	billion cubic feet
Btu	British thermal unit
°F	degree Fahrenheit
MMcf	million cubic feet
%	percent
psia	pounds per square inch, absolute
Tcf	trillion cubic feet

Suggested citation:

Gage, B.D. and D.L. Driskill. 2004. Helium resources of the United States–2003, Technical Note 415
Bureau of Land Management. Denver, Colorado. BLM/NM/ST-04/002+3745. 40 pp.

Contents

Figures

Tables

Abstract

This report deviates from previous reports in defining helium reserves. It includes only the estimated helium contained in fields and formations from which helium is currently being recovered. The Cliffside Gasfield is expected to continue to be used to deliver the helium needed to meet worldwide demand. Figure 6 shows the possible demand, using set criteria, for the helium stored in the Cliffside Gasfield to meet helium sales.

The identified helium resources of the United States are estimated at 449 Bcf as of December 31, 2002. This includes 131 Bcf of demonstrated reserves, 132 Bcf of demonstrated marginal reserves, and 37 Bcf of demonstrated subeconomic resources. The identified resources also include 149 Bcf of helium in inferred subeconomic resources. The demonstrated helium resources contained on Federal lands are approximately 150 Bcf, including 29 Bcf in underground storage in the Cliffside Gasfield near Amarillo, Texas. In addition to the identified helium resources, undiscovered helium resources in the United States are estimated at a most likely volume of 108 Bcf, with a maximum volume of 292 Bcf and a minimum volume of 44 Bcf. Also reported are 56 Bcf of helium in nonconventional and low helium content natural gases.

Current extraction of helium in the United States occurs mostly from natural gases produced from the Hugoton gas area in Kansas, Oklahoma, and Texas, and the Riley Ridge area in southwestern Wyoming. Helium extracted from natural gas in the United States in 2002 was approximately 3.1 Bcf, with additional production of stored helium from the Cliffside Gasfield of 1.4 Bcf. The volume of helium produced with the natural gas in the Hugoton gas area continues to decline. The trend continues to be the withdrawal from the Cliffside Gasfield of privately owned crude helium by private industry. The open market sale of the Government's helium initiated in 2003 allows for the transfer of the Government owned helium to private industry. The helium sales from the mid-continent remained basically flat from 2000 to 2002. The helium market has not grown at the recent historical rates of 5.7 percent annually from 1995 to 2000. The helium sales forecast for the future is not clear at this time. Additional helium is expected to come into the market from plants in Algeria and Qatar during 2005. The helium extracted from natural gas produced in the mid-continent is estimated to be declining at 10 percent annually.

Introduction

The identified helium resources of the United States are estimated at 449 Bcf.[1] This includes both demonstrated and inferred helium contained in proved, probable, and possible natural gas resources.[2] It also includes helium previously separated from natural gases and stored at the Cliffside Gasfield in Potter County, Texas. The helium contained in other occurrences of natural gas in the United States is estimated at 56 Bcf; this includes helium in nonconventional gas reserves and low-helium-content natural gas. The undiscovered helium resources in the United States are estimated at a most likely value of 108 Bcf. This results in a total helium resource base of 613 Bcf.

This publication is the 13th in a series of reports on the helium resources of the Nation. The first of these reports gave information on helium resources as of January 1, 1973 (1).[3] The reports have been published approximately every 2 years with the last Technical Note reporting information as of December 31, 2000 (2-12). It has been 3 years since the last update to this publication. The graph in Figure 6 estimates the helium production needed from the Cliffside Gasfield to meet helium demand. The graph is an indicator, but is very simplistic in nature and cannot be expected to account for the many events that control sales growth or decline.

This office has been estimating the Nation's helium resources for about 55 years in connection with a search for helium occurrences that has been conducted for over 80 years. These activities are carried on: (1) to ensure a continuing supply of helium to fill essential Federal needs, (2) to provide information to the Secretary of the Interior so that helium resources reserved to the United States on Federal land can be properly managed, and (3) to provide the public with information on a limited natural resource that is being depleted.

The Mineral Lands Leasing Act of 1920 reserves to the United States all helium found on Federal lands leased under the provisions of that Act. The responsibility for ensuring a supply of helium to meet essential Federal needs was assigned to the Secretary of the Interior by the Helium Act of March 31, 1925. This was followed by the Helium Act Amendments of 1960, which among other things, allowed the Secretary of the Interior to purchase crude helium for storage at the Cliffside Field. The latest legislation pertaining to helium is the Helium Privatization Act of 1996. The helium resource estimates and supply/demand forecasts presented in this report are realistic for the short term; however, as in all long-term forecasts, less reliance should be placed on the estimates toward the end of the forecast.

---

[1] All values in this report, unless otherwise stated, are at 14.65 psia and 60 °F as of December 31, 2002.

[2] See Glossary for definitions of resource terms.

[3] The numbers in parentheses refer to items in the list of references near the end of this report.

The estimate of the total helium resource base of 613 Bcf is less than the 631 Bcf estimated as of December 31, 2000. The decrease is primarily due to changes in estimates of natural gas resources by the Potential Gas Committee (PGC) (13). The identified resources are classified based on degree of geological assurance of occurrence. This classification results in the categories termed measured, indicated, and inferred resources. See the Glossary for definitions of these terms and their relationship to the oil and gas industry terms of proved, probable, and possible. Measured resources, including storage, are 195 Bcf; indicated resources are 105 Bcf; and inferred resources are 149 Bcf.

The identified helium resources can be subdivided into three categories (Figure 1): (1) reserves containing 131 Bcf, which includes helium in underground storage; (2) marginal reserves containing 132 Bcf; and (3) subeconomic resources containing 186 Bcf. The helium resource base also includes approximately 56 Bcf of helium in other natural gas occurrences. These natural gas occurrences include coalbed methane and natural gases with very low helium content, generally less than 0.05 percent. The undiscovered helium resources comprise the remainder of the

helium resource base, and the estimate, 108 Bcf, is based on the most likely speculative gas resource values provided by the PGC. The minimum value for the undiscovered resources is 44 Bcf and the maximum value is 292 Bcf. The definitions for the helium and natural gas resource terms are found in the Glossary. The definitions and uses of the terms in this Technical Note follow the general guidelines established by the United States Geological Survey as published in USGS Bulletin 1450-A, *Principles of the Mineral Resource Classification System of the United States Bureau of Mines and the United States Geological Survey, 1976*, and later revised in Geological Circular 831, 1980.

This report categorizes the resources on an economic basis. The helium content of the gases is an economic consideration because the extraction costs generally decrease as helium content increases. However, other factors that affect the economic potential of helium deposits are also considered and included in classifying helium resources. These factors include the average daily rate of processed gas, helium content of natural gas, hydrocarbon recovery, life of the reserves, size of the reserves, and proximity to the Government's helium storage system.

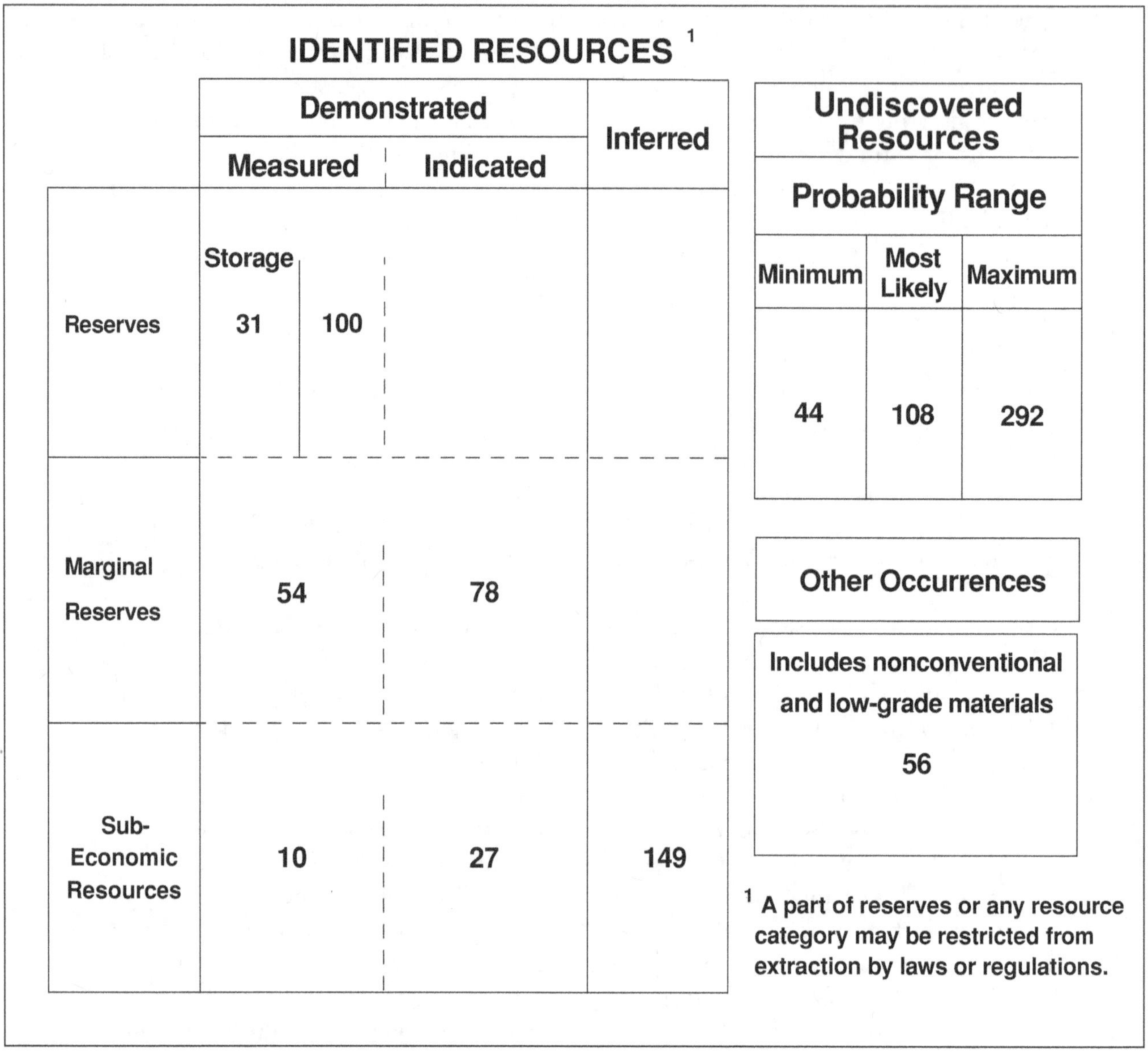

IDENTIFIED RESOURCES [1]

	Demonstrated		Inferred
	Measured	**Indicated**	
Reserves	Storage 31 100		
Marginal Reserves	54	78	
Sub-Economic Resources	10	27	149

Undiscovered Resources

Probability Range

Minimum	Most Likely	Maximum
44	108	292

Other Occurrences

Includes nonconventional and low-grade materials

56

[1] A part of reserves or any resource category may be restricted from extraction by laws or regulations.

Figure 1. Identified and undiscovered helium resources in the United States (billion cubic feet at 14.65 psia and 60 °F). Modified from *Principles of a Resource/Reserve Classification of Minerals* (Geological Survey Circular 831, 1980).

Identified Helium Resources

Helium occurs as a constituent of natural gas, which is presently the only economical source, and helium is also present in the atmosphere. For this report, helium in the atmosphere is not considered as part of the helium resource base. The natural gas in which helium is found may be normal fuel gas; naturally occurring, low-Btu gas; or nonconventional gas resources such as coalbed methane and carbon dioxide gas. The helium content of the natural gas resources is derived from Bureau of Land Management (BLM) records of helium analyses of natural gas samples, which are a part of the BLM's resource database. The analysis of natural gas and limited evaluations of helium resources started in 1917. Over 21,100 natural gas samples from wells and pipelines in the United States and other countries have been analyzed through 2001, and 16,369 of these analyses have been documented in 43 publications. These publications are listed in the bibliography of this report.

Helium in Storage

In 1961, the Government contracted to purchase helium from five extraction plants built by four private companies adjacent to large natural gas transmission pipelines. The gas, principally from the West Panhandle and Hugoton Gasfields in the Texas and Oklahoma Panhandles and in southwestern Kansas, was being produced for fuel. As the gas was burned, the helium was released to the atmosphere and wasted. Using private funds, these companies constructed plants to extract crude helium for sale to the Government. The helium was delivered into a Government-owned pipeline that connected all plants with the Bush Dome in the Cliffside Gasfield near Amarillo, Texas. Further information concerning the Government's helium purchases can be found in the first report of this series (1) and the section in this report on the history and uses of helium.

Bush Dome was the source of helium-bearing natural gas that was produced for helium extraction at the Government's Amarillo Helium Plant from 1929 until the plant ceased helium extraction operations in April 1970. About 110 Bcf of natural gas has been produced from the field and there are about 200 Bcf of remaining recoverable gas reserves. The natural gas averages about 1.86 percent contained helium; therefore, the remaining native helium reserves are about 3.7 Bcf. Since the Amarillo Helium Plant ceased helium extraction operations, natural gas has been produced from Bush Dome for fuel. The addition of the Crude Helium Enrichment Unit in 2003 created a means to increase the helium percent of the crude-helium stream going into the Government's conservation pipeline and to sell the hydrocarbons as a byproduct of this process.

The Helium Privatization Act of 1996 mandated the cessation of the operation of the Exell Helium Plant, with private industry supplying helium to Federal agencies using in-kind crude helium sales contracts. Helium contained in the remaining native gas is included with the helium in the measured helium reserves. As of December 31, 2002, the helium stored in Bush Dome totaled 30.8 Bcf. Of this total, 29.2 Bcf was accepted by the Government from the conservation plants under contract and was excess to Federal market demands. The other 1.6 Bcf is stored by the Government for private companies under separate storage contracts.

Other Measured Helium Resources

The demonstrated, measured helium reserves and resources are considered the most accurate estimates of this report and are 164 Bcf, not including storage and other occurrences of helium. The measured helium is subdivided into reserves, marginal reserves, and subeconomic resources. Presently, all measured reserves are in helium-rich natural gas. The marginal reserves and subeconomic helium resources are contained in both helium-rich and helium-lean natural gas. All gasfields known to contain at least 0.05 percent helium have been individually evaluated and are part of the demonstrated helium resources. Fields containing less than 0.05 percent helium are not individually evaluated. The helium resources in these fields are estimated by using average helium contents of natural gas from representative fields and basins and applying those values to the Department of Energy/Energy Information Administration (DOE/EIA) reserve estimates (14). These helium resources, although they are contained in proved natural gas reserves, are reported as other occurrences of helium.

Measured Helium Reserves

The measured helium reserves are estimated at 100 Bcf, excluding storage. These reserves are located in 11 gas-producing areas in eight States. The reserves by State and area are listed in Table 1. The locations are shown in Figure 2.

Since 1950, the Federal Government has been making estimates of the helium resources of the Nation, although for several years the estimates included only the fields that contained major deposits of at least 0.30 percent helium. These fields were the Hugoton in southwestern Kansas and the Oklahoma and Texas Panhandles, the West Panhandle in Texas, the Greenwood in Kansas, the Keyes in Oklahoma, and the Cliffside Field in Texas. Even today these fields are estimated to contain approximately 31 percent, or 31 Bcf, of the measured helium reserves. The natural gas from all these fields is being produced for fuel, and the helium that is not extracted is lost to the atmosphere as the natural gas is burned.

As the helium resources evaluation program in the United States progressed, more comprehensive data were collected and the estimates were improved. In 1961,

Table 1. Measured helium reserves. Volumes are in MMcf at 14.65 psia and 60 °F, as of December 31, 2002.

State	Area	Helium Reserves	Federally Owned	Marginal Helium Reserves	Federally Owned	Subeconomic Helium Resources	Federally Owned
Arizona	Apache County	385	0	189	0		
Arkansas	Arkansas Valley					1,410	107
Colorado	Baca County			162	4		
	Douglas Crk Arch			192	187	176	169
	Paradox Basin	194	194			3,885	2,995
	Miscellaneous			254	165		
	Las Animas Arch	660	0				
Total Colorado		854	194	608	356	4,061	3,164
Kansas	Hugoton (Fields in South West Kansas)	24,002	835				
	Other Areas			423	0	449	20
Total Kansas		24,002	835	423	0	449	20
Montana	Rudyard/Utopia			189	0		
	Other Areas					881	123
New Mexico	Chaves County			1,587	1,000		
	Northwest NM	180	0	627	24		
Total New Mexico		180	0	2,214	1,024		
Oklahoma	Guymon Hugoton	1,741	10				
	Keyes Gas Area	420	6				
	Other Areas					1,175	5
Total Oklahoma		2,161	16			1,175	5
Texas	Cliffside Area Native Gas	3,742	3,742				
	District 10	6,770	16				
	Other Areas					1,019	6
Total Texas		10,512	3,758			1,019	6
Utah	Lisbon Area	747	660				
	Other Areas			1,215	1,029	155	79
Total Utah		747	660	1,215	1,029	155	79
Wyoming	Riley Ridge	60,931	56,726	46,923	44,113		
	Church Buttes Area			1,432	729		
	Washakie Basin			1,200	749	311	108
Total Wyoming		60,931	56,726	49,555	45,591	311	108
Miscellaneous States						49	0
Total United States		**99,772**	**62,189**	**54,393**	**48,000**	**9,510**	**3,612**

a major improvement in the program took place when, for the first time, helium reserves were estimated for all fields in the United States from which samples containing more than 0.30 percent helium had been analyzed in connection with the gas-sampling program. Available data for many of these smaller fields were limited for the first evaluation efforts; however, over the intervening years, data has been collected from all known, available sources. This has resulted in a comprehensive assessment of the total helium resources of the country.

Before the implementation of crude helium purchases in late 1961, all of the previously mentioned gasfields with large helium reserves were being produced for fuel. The resultant loss of helium amounted to

approximately 8 Bcf per year. Under the crude helium purchase program, approximately 3.5 Bcf of helium, that otherwise would have been wasted, was saved annually from 1962 through November 12, 1973, when the Government ceased the purchase of helium from the private conservation plants.

Some of the gasfields that contain measured reserves of helium are not being produced, and the helium is not being wasted. These are classified as nondepleting helium reserves. There are 42 fields in seven States that are nondepleting. These nondepleting fields contain marginal reserves and subeconomic resources of helium. Table 2 lists the nondepleting and depleting resources by category.

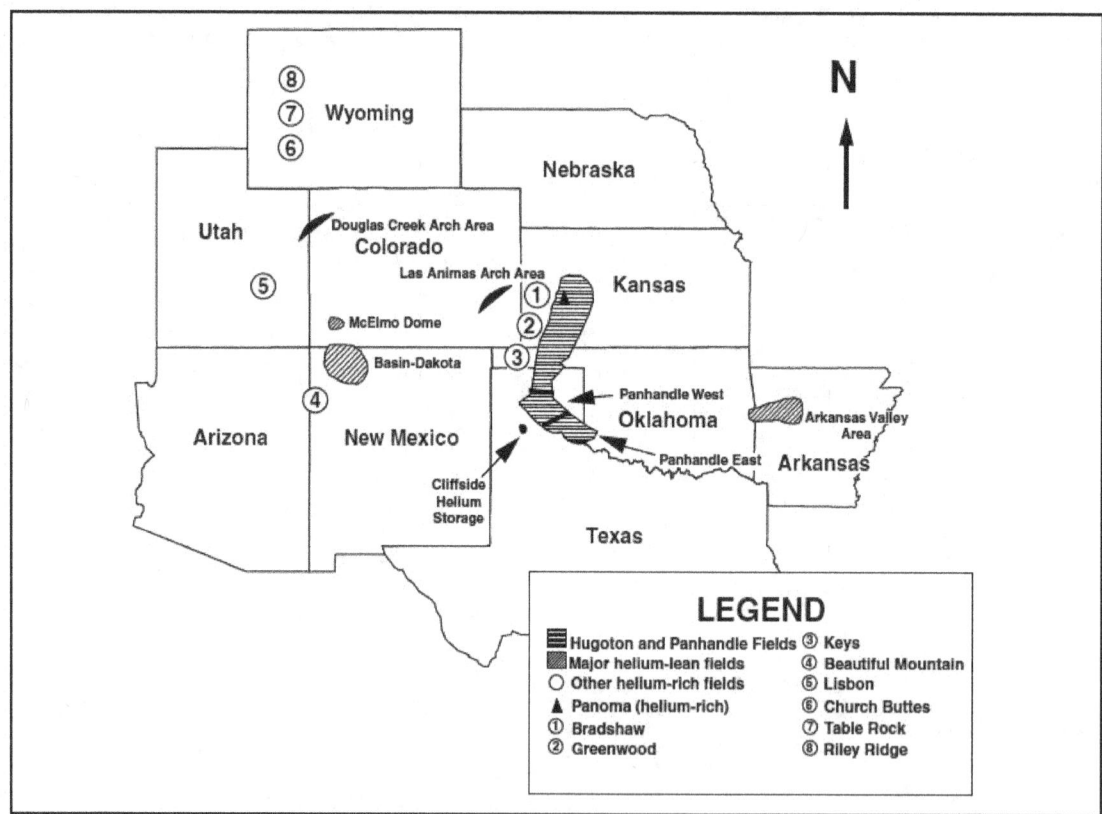

Figure 2. Location of major helium-bearing gasfields.

Table 2. Depleting and nondepleting demonstrated helium reserves and resources. Volumes in Bcf at 14.65 psia and 60 °F.

	Depleting	Federal	Nondepleting	Federal
Measured Reserves[1]	100	62	<1	0
Indicated Reserves	0	0	0	0
Measured Marginal Reserves	2	1	52	47
Indicated Marginal Reserves	72	<1	6	3
Measured Subeconomic Resources	9	4	1	<1
Indicated Subeconomic Resources	27	<1	0	0
Total	210	67	59	50

[1] Does not include 31 Bcf in storage, of which 29 Bcf is owned by the Federal Government.

There are various reasons why these fields are not being produced. Some are located in remote areas where pipeline connections are not presently available. In other cases, the gas is being used in pressure maintenance operations to produce associated oil. In the majority of these fields, however, the helium is in natural gas that has a low heating value and thus is not suitable for fuel. Fields in the first two groups will be put on production eventually, and the helium reserves moved to the depleting category. For example, the Lisbon Field in southeastern Utah had been under pressure maintenance and secondary recovery operations since 1969, when gas production operations began. In conjunction with the gas production, helium extraction capabilities were added and helium recovery began during 1994. As natural gas prices rise, some of the fields with low-heating value gas will be produced. In 1986, one major field in this group, Riley Ridge in Sublette County, Wyoming, began production from the Madison Formation. This transferred approximately 71 Bcf of helium from the nondepleting to the depleting category of measured helium reserves.

The Mineral Lands Leasing Act of 1920 reserves to the United States all helium found on Federal lands leased under the provisions of that Act. In this report, the term "Federal lands" applies to those lands on which the Government owns the gas rights. Under these provisions, the United States is estimated to own 91 Bcf of helium found in measured helium reserves on Federal lands. The measured helium reserves are comprised of 91 Bcf of depleting reserves (Table 2).

Measured Marginal Helium Reserves

The measured marginal helium reserves are approximately 54 Bcf. These marginal reserves are found in 12 gas-producing areas in seven States (Table 1). A portion of these marginal helium reserves are found in different geologic formations in fields also containing measured helium reserves or in proximity to these reserves. They are classified as marginal helium reserves primarily based on the expectation that an improvement in economics may result in extraction of helium. (Appendix A).

Helium-rich gasfields account for all of the measured marginal helium reserves. These resources are classified as marginal reserves because of their small size, generally less than 0.5 Bcf of helium. In the future, it is possible that helium may be extracted from these formations.

Measured Subeconomic Helium Resources

This category is made up of both helium-rich and helium-lean gasfields. Each helium-rich gasfield containing less than 150 MMcf of helium, and each helium-lean gasfield containing more than 150 MMcf and less than 1 Bcf of helium is included, with the exception of McElmo Dome in southwestern Colorado, which contains approximately 4 Bcf of helium. The gas composition in the McElmo Dome is mainly carbon dioxide with a helium content of 0.07 percent, which makes it unlikely that helium will ever be extracted. The measured subeconomic helium resources are estimated at approximately 10 Bcf. Nearly all of these resources are depleting and most are in helium-lean gasfields, with less than 0.5 Bcf in helium-rich gasfields. The helium resources are listed by State in Table 1. Although it is possible to extract helium

from gasfields in this category, it is unlikely. These gasfields are isolated from current helium extraction facilities and contain small amounts of helium.

The Arkansas Valley Area is placed in the subeconomic resources, although the application of the category criteria would place it in the marginal helium reserves. It is considered unlikely that extraction of helium from the natural gas will ever happen. The helium content of the natural gas is approximately 0.11 percent, and nitrogen rejection is not necessary.

Indicated Helium Resources

The indicated helium resources of the United States are 78 Bcf of marginal reserves and 27 Bcf in subeconomic resources. The indicated helium resources are derived from the PGC's estimate of probable resources of natural gas. The average helium contents are estimated for each PGC region or basin and used to determine the amount of indicated helium in each basin. See Figure 3 for a general map of PGC regions. The assumption is that probable gas resources in a basin will contain similar gases and helium content as proven gas reserves. However, new discoveries may contain significantly higher helium contents than previously found in a particular basin. In addition, some basins contain indicated helium that has been evaluated in conjunction with individual gasfield evaluations. This helium is included as part of the PGC-derived value, not added to it, except low-Btu gases that are not included in the PGC's estimate.

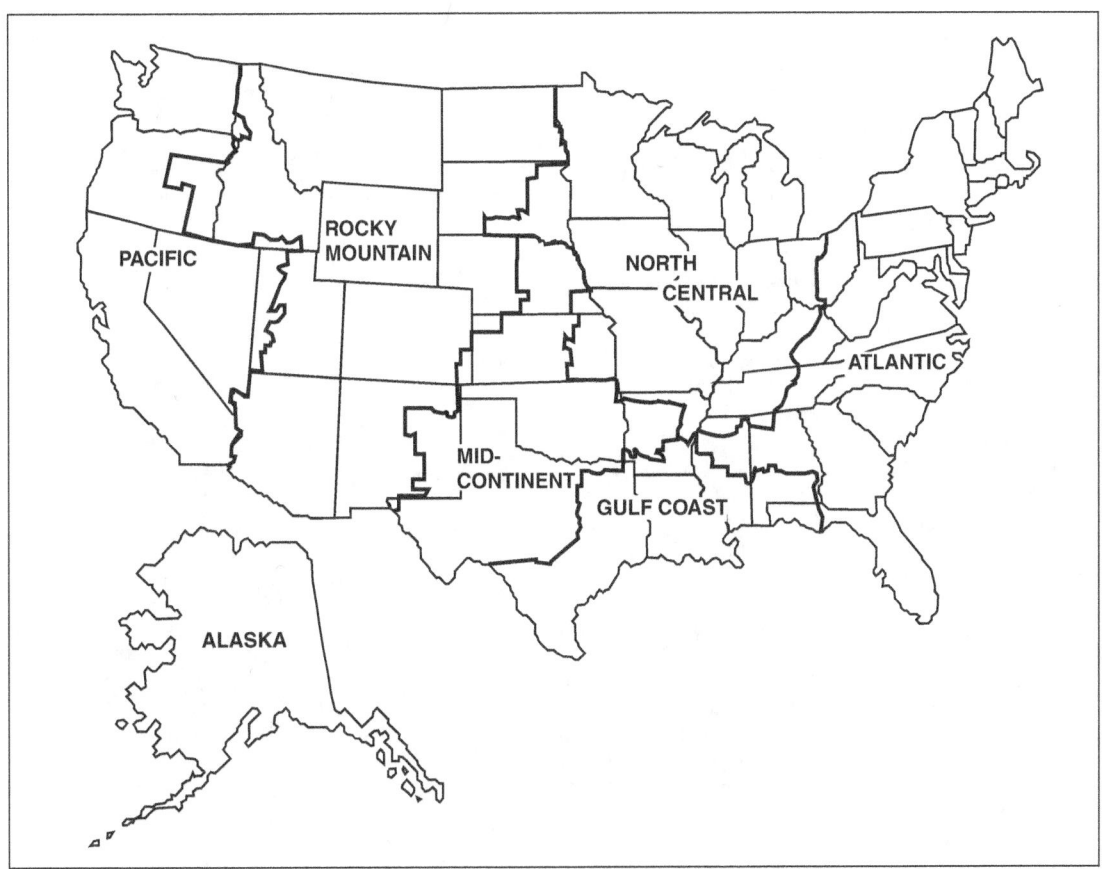

Figure 3. Map of potential Gas Committee (PGC) Regions.

There are no indicated helium reserves carried in the helium reserves category.

The indicated marginal helium reserves contain 72 Bcf of depleting helium and 6 Bcf of nondepleting helium.[4] Only about 3 Bcf of this is known to be on Federal land. The indicated subeconomic resources are all in depleting reservoirs and less than 1 Bcf is known to be on Federal land.

Approximately 6 Bcf of the indicated helium is associated with individually evaluated gasfields. The 6 Bcf is contained in marginal helium reserves. The remainder, 99 Bcf of the indicated resources, is derived from the PGC's probable gas resources estimates. Because more importance is placed on reserves and marginal reserves, only gasfields containing helium reserves and marginal helium reserves are individually

---

[4] Technically, all indicated helium is nondepleating since these resources are not developed or actually producing. The terms "depleting" and "nondepleting" as used here show that the helium is associated with currently depleting or nondepleting fields.

Table 3. Estimated average helium contents of gas resources by PGC region and basin.

Region and Basin			Avg. Helium Content	Footnotes
Alaska			0.0111%	1
Atlantic:	P-100	New England and Adirondack Uplifts	0.0233%	1
	P-110	Atlantic Coastal Basin	0.0233%	1
	P-120	Appalachian Basin	0.0497%	1
	P-130	Piedmont-Blue Ridge Province	0.0497%	1
	P-140	South Georgia-Peninsular Florida	0.0150%	1
	P-150	Black Warrior Basin	0.0100%	1
Gulf Coast:	P-300	Louisiana-Mississippi-Alabama Salt Dome	0.0430%	1
	P-310	Louisiana Gulf Coast Basin	0.0020%	1
	P-320	East Texas Basin	0.0017%	1
	P-330	Texas Gulf Coast Basin	0.0020%	1
	P-930	Eastern Gulf Shelf	0.0014%	2
	P-931	Eastern Gulf Slope	0.0014%	1
	P-935	Louisiana Shelf	0.0014%	2
	P-936	Louisiana Slope	0.0014%	2
	P-940	Texas Shelf	0.0014%	2
	P-941	Texas Slope	0.0014%	2
	P-945	Gulf of Mexico Outer Continental Slope	0.0014%	1
Mid-continent:	P-400	Central Kansas Uplift, Salina Basin	0.2081%	1
	P-410	Arkoma Basin	0.0110%	1
	P-420	Anadarko, Palo Duro Basins, etc.	0.2081%	1
	P-430	Fort Worth and Strawn Basins, Bend Arch	0.2550%	1
	P-440	Permian Basin	0.0282%	1
North Central			0.0371%	1
Pacific			0.0069%	1
Rocky Mountain:	P-500	Williston Basin	0.0802%	1
	P-510	Powder River Basin	0.0793%	1
	P-515	Big Horn Basin	0.0490%	1
	P-520	Wind River Basin	0.0417%	1
	P-530	Greater Green River Basin < 15,000 ft	0.0760%	1
	P-530	Greater Green River Basin > 15,000 ft	0.5190%	3
	P-535	Denver Basin, Chadron Arch and Las Animas Arch	0.0642%	1
	P-540	Uinta/Piceance Basins; Park and Eagle Basins	0.1720%	1
	P-545	San Juan Mountains; San Louis and Raton Basins	0.0230%	2
	P-550	Paradox Basin	0.4150%	1
	P-555	San Juan Basin	0.0228%	1
	P-560	Southern Basin and Range Province	0.0150%	2
	P-565	Plateau Province, Black Mesa Basin	0.0070%	2
	P-570	Sweetgrass Arch	0.1602%	1
	P-575	Montana Folded Belt	0.1602%	1
	P-580	Snake River Basin	0.0275%	1
	P-590	Wyoming-Utah-Idaho Thrust Belt	0.0824%	1

FOOTNOTES:

1. The average helium content is weighted based on the number of gas samples from each formation and field combination in the region.

2. The average helium content is derived from pipeline gas surveys carried out by the Bureau and is weighted based on gas volumes flowing through gas plants in the region.

3. The average helium content is weighted heavily to the high helium-bearing gas in the Riley Ridge field. The helium contents of other gases in the area also are considered.

Table 4. Estimated indicated helium resources by PGC basin. All volumes are in Bcf at 14.65 psia and 60 °F.

PGC Basin		Reserves	Marginal Reserves	Subeconomic Resources
P-530	Greater Green River Basin >15,000'			
P-550	Paradox Basin		2.09	
P-400	Central Kansas Uplift, Salina Basin		0.37	
P-420	Anadarko, Palo Duro Basins, etc.		42.96	
P-430	Ft. Worth and Strawn Basins, Bend Arch			5.95
P-540	Uinta, Piceance Basins		26.06	
P-570	Sweetgrass Arch			0.70
P-120	Appalachian Basin			9.87
P-500	Williston Basin			0.53
P-510	Powder River Basin			1.14
P-515	Big Horn Basin			0.41
P-530	Greater Green River Basin<15,000'			6.60
P-535	Denver Basin, Chadron Arch			0.89
P-590	Wyoming-Utah-Idaho Thrust Belt			0.66
	Total	0	71.48	26.75

evaluated for indicated resources. In the subeconomic category, all indicated resource estimates are derived from the PGC probable gas resource values.

Table 3 shows projections for the average helium contents of gas resources by PGC region and basin. The estimated indicated helium resources for each PGC area have been placed in a resource category based on size and helium content. The same criteria used in determining resource placement for the measured reserves are applied to the indicated resources. These resource estimates are shown in Table 4.

Inferred Helium Resources

The inferred helium resources of the United States are 149 Bcf in subeconomic resources. The inferred helium resources are derived from the PGC's estimate of possible gas resources. As with indicated helium resources, estimates are made of the average helium contents of the possible gas resources for the PGC areas and basins. The average helium contents are based on helium contents of proven reserves and all areas that have potential for significant helium finds in the future. Every basin and area studied, with the exceptions of the Gulf Coast and

Table 5. Estimated inferred helium resources by PGC basin. All volumes are in Bcf at 14.65 psia and 60 °F.

PGC	Basin or Region	Reserves	Marginal Reserves	Subeconomic Resources
P-530	Greater Green River Basin>15,000'			29.72
P-550	Paradox Basin			4.17
P-400	Central Kansas Uplift, Salina Basin			0.29
P-420	Anadarko, Palo Duro Basins, etc.			43.83
P-430	Ft. Worth and Strawn Basins, Bend Arch			4.69
P-540	Uinta, Piceance Basins			26.15
P-570	Sweetgrass Arch			1.52
P-575	Montana Folded Belt			6.44
	Alaska			1.83
P-120	Appalachian Basin			3.65
P-150	Black Warrior Basin			0.07
	Gulf Coast Region (on and offshore)			4.01
P-410	Arkoma Basin			0.14
P-440	Permian Basin			5.43
	North Central Region			1.37
	Pacific Region			1.52
P-500	Williston Basin			0.83
P-510	Powder River Basin			1.72
P-515	Big Horn Basin			0.56
P-520	Wind River Basin			3.31
P-530	Greater Green River Basin <15,000'			4.54
P-535	Denver Basin, Chadron Arch			0.65
P-545	San Juan Mtns, San Louis/Raton Basin			0.09
P-555	San Juan Basin			1.48
P-560	Southern Basin and Range Province			0.21
P-590	Wyoming-Utah-Idaho Thrust Belt			0.83
	Total	0	0	149.05

the Pacific areas, have contained some helium-rich natural gas. Possible Federal ownership of the inferred resources was not estimated. Table 5 shows the estimated inferred helium resources for each PGC basin/region and the category in which the resources are placed.

The PGC's possible gas resources are placed in the subeconomic category. The probable resources are based on extension of productive fields and are more certain than the possible gas resources. The possible resources are a less assured supply because they are postulated to exist outside known fields, but are associated with a productive formation in a productive province. The

possible resources were entered into the identified resources under the inferred resources of the subeconomic resources of Figure 1. The PGC possible resources will be updated as more information becomes available on the areas. For this reason, less reliance should be put on the helium resources of these areas until gas production is proven by development of new fields. Although the Federal Government has fields with helium content in the areas covered by the PGC, it is difficult to assign anything other than subeconomic to the postulated resources. This is done to keep from giving an overly optimistic estimate of the helium associated with these possible future fields.

Other Helium Occurrences

Other occurrences of helium include helium contained in nonconventional natural gas and extremely lean (low-grade) helium occurrences. All proven reserves of natural gas that contain less than 0.05 percent helium are in this category. In addition, helium in coalbed methane and some carbon dioxide occurrences are also included. The helium resources in other occurrences are about 56 Bcf.

An average helium content is applied to the DOE/EIA reserves of natural gas less the evaluated natural gasfields containing measured helium to arrive at a value for helium contained in the remaining gas reserves. The average helium contents are derived from the helium survey analyses of gas wells and past surveys of gas transmission pipelines and are weighted based on flow through the pipelines. The total helium in other occurrences from this source is about 32 Bcf.

Other occurrences of helium are the coalbed methane resources and some carbon dioxide resources. The BLM has estimated that the coalbed methane contains about 6 Bcf of helium. The reserves reported by the EIA for coalbed methane in the United States were used to determine the estimated helium associated with coalbed methane. The helium resources in the carbon dioxide gases of the Sheep Mountain area of Colorado are less than 1 Bcf. Other carbon dioxide producing fields have significant helium contents and are categorized as helium reserves, marginal reserves (Riley Ridge Field), and subeconomic resources (McElmo Dome Field) as previously discussed.

Additionally, certain evaluated fields containing helium-lean natural gas are contained in this category. These fields generally contain small amounts of helium and are remote from major gas transmission lines. These miscellaneous fields contain about 3 Bcf of helium.

The last source of helium in this category is from certain estimates for the resource category designated as probable gas resources by the PGC (Table 4). Basins and areas that contain probable gas resources with average helium contents of less than 0.05 percent are also placed in the other occurrences category and contain approximately 14 Bcf of helium. Table 6 lists all estimates of helium in other occurrences.

Table 6. Helium in other occurrences. Volumes in Bcf at 14.65 psia and 60 °F.

Category	Occurrence
Coalbed methane	
Black Warrior Basin	6.47
CO_2 Resources	
Colorado/New Mexico	0.68
DOE/EIA	32.36
Miscellaneous	2.69
From PGC-Probable:	
Alaska	3.44
P-150 Black Warrior Basin	0.05
Gulf Coast Region	2.76
P-410 Arkoma Basin	0.28
P-440 Permian Basin	3.12
North Central Region	0.74
Pacific Region	0.27
P-520 Wind River Basin	1.53
P-555 San Juan Basin	1.32
Total	55.71

Undiscovered Helium Resources

The undiscovered helium resources in the United States are estimated at a most likely value of 108 Bcf, with a minimum value of 44 Bcf, and a maximum value of 292 Bcf. The estimates are based on the PGC's minimum, most likely, and maximum speculative gas resources combined with the BLM's estimate of average helium contents. The same average helium contents that are used for indicated and inferred helium resources are used for undiscovered resources. No attempt was made to estimate the minimum and maximum helium contents because for most basins the helium contents fall within a very narrow range of values. For example, analyses of gases from the offshore Gulf Coast area have never indicated helium contents greater than 0.05 percent. In areas, such as the mid-continent, where the helium contents have a wider range of values, statistical analyses showed no pattern to the helium contents based on size of reservoir or discovery. Further, studies of proven gas reserves by basin, reservoir, and helium contents (15) show that gases in most basins and reservoirs contain helium contents within a narrow range of values. New discoveries within these basins tend to follow the helium content pattern of past discoveries.

Production and Extraction

Background

The Federal Government's role in helium dates to World War I when the Army and Navy became interested in using helium as an inert lifting gas and contacted the Bureau of Mines (BOM) for assistance because of its natural gas expertise. The Helium Act of 1925 officially placed the helium program under Government control. The BOM built a large-scale helium extraction and purification facility and began operations in 1929. During World War II, demand increased significantly and four more small Government plants were built.

Increased helium demand in the 1950s led to construction of the Keyes, Oklahoma, helium plant in 1959. Dwindling mid-continent natural gas supplies aroused concerns that no economic source of helium would exist by the turn of the century and led to the passage of amendments to the Helium Act of 1925. The Helium Act Amendments of 1960 provided for the conservation of helium for essential Government needs and also was intended to promote the development of a private helium industry. The Act directed the Secretary of the Interior to purchase and store helium for future use and to maintain helium production and purification plants and related helium storage, transmission, and shipping facilities.

Purchases for the conservation program were made from private companies, which added crude helium extraction plants to existing gas processing facilities. The BOM built a high-pressure pipeline to transport the helium from Bushton, Kansas, and intermediate points, to the government-owned Cliffside Gasfield for storage. In 1973, the contracts with private companies were canceled because the Secretary determined that the long-term needs of the Government were adequately fulfilled. In 1975, the Government began accepting privately owned crude helium for storage at the Cliffside Gasfield. As of December 31, 2002, private industry had about 1.6 Bcf of helium stored at Cliffside.

Helium Privatization Act of 1996

On October 9, 1996, the President signed the Helium Privatization Act of 1996 (Public Law 104-273). This legislation directed the Government to cease the production and sale of refined helium on April 9, 1998. Some of the key components of this legislation include:

- The disposal of all helium production, refining, and sales-related assets not later than 24 months after the closure of the helium refinery.

  Status: A historical review was initiated in June 1999, and reports were completed in August 1999. The Phase 1 environmental site assessment was initiated in early 1999, and reports were completed in July 1999. The National Park Service (NPS) completed the historic structures inventory for the Amarillo and Exell plants in 1999. The Landis Property was accepted into the Texas Voluntary Cleanup Program (VCP) during 2000. The Phase II archeological testing was completed for the Landis Property in 2000. Phase II environmental site assessment work plans and initial characterization sampling were completed for the Landis Property in 2001. Through cooperation with the General Services Administration, final disposition of personal properties was completed during 2000. The Amarillo Helium Plant was accepted into the VCP during 2001. The Amarillo Helium Plant did not require onsite remediation, based on characterization sampling.

A draft of the historical architectural engineering report was prepared by NPS for the Exell and Amarillo plants. The final characterization and delineation sampling was completed in 2002, and laboratory results were submitted to the Texas Commission on Environmental Quality.

- Offer for sale the Federal reserves of crude helium in excess of 600 MMcf to begin no later than January 1, 2005, and complete sales by January 1, 2015.

   Status: Crude helium sales (in-kind) for helium that is sold to Federal agencies and their contractors by private companies began in January 1998. The in-kind helium sales were 225 MMcf in 2002. The open market sales of Government-owned helium were initiated in March 2003, with 1,640 MMcf of helium sold. A second sale took place in October 2003 with 676 MMcf of helium sold. Future open market sales will take place to correspond with the Government's fiscal year, which starts in October.

- Continue operation of the helium storage field and conservation pipeline for storage and distribution of crude helium. This component is to meet private industry and Government needs using in-kind crude helium sales contracts with private suppliers. Private companies also have bought Government helium through open market sales to meet the helium demand of their customers.

- Continue the collection of helium royalty and fee sales for helium extracted from Federal lands.

- Continue helium resource evaluation and reserve tracking to monitor helium availability for essential Government programs.

Uses of Helium

Helium is chemically inert, which means that no other element will combine with helium at any temperature or pressure. Helium is the second lightest element, with hydrogen being the lightest. Helium liquifies at approximately -452 °F, making it useful in cryogenics, the study of the behavior of matter and energy at temperatures below -270 °F. The properties possessed by helium make it an element that can be used in a variety of applications.

Since helium will not burn or react with other substances, it is used to shield reactive metals, such as aluminum, from contamination by other elements during arc welding. The inert characteristics of helium keep it from reacting in the body, which allows it to be used in breathing mixtures supplied to some undersea explorers and operating-room patients. Helium is seven times lighter than air and noncombustible, thus making it applicable as the lifting gas inside high-altitude weather and research balloons and lighter-than-air craft.

Helium is used to control atmospheric conditions in special chambers where silicon crystals used in electronic applications are grown. The production of fiber-optic wire requires an ultra-pure inert atmosphere. Helium's immunity to radioactivity led to its use as a heat transfer medium in gas-cooled nuclear power reactors. The molecular size of helium allows it to escape through the tiniest holes, which makes helium useful for detecting leaks during the manufacture of sealed fluid systems like those used in refrigerators and vacuum systems. The very low temperature at which helium liquifies causes certain metals to become superconductors losing all resistance to the flow of electricity. This has made possible the construction of powerful magnets that can be used to monitor physical and chemical conditions inside the human body, and to accelerate subatomic particles to velocities near the speed of light for experiments in high-energy physics.

The development of liquid-fueled rockets increased the uses for helium in space exploration and missile technology. The Atlas, Saturn V, and Space Shuttle have applied the technology developed for helium for use in space travel. The fuel tanks of all these spacecraft are pressurized by helium to push the fuel into the pumps feeding the rocket engines and to provide pressure, enabling thin-walled tanks to resist collapse when empty. The Space Shuttle also uses helium in the orbital maneuvering system engines that enable the shuttle to change the shape and altitude of its orbit.

Other evolving technologies that require the unique properties of helium are: (1) metastable helium for energy storage, which involves raising helium electrons to an excited energy state and then stabilizing the atom; (2) helium ion tumor treatment, where large inert particles are required; (3) liquid helium-cooled superconducting microswitches, called Josephson junctions, which are much faster than conventional semiconductors and use less power; and (4) "aneutronic" nuclear fusion of deuterium and helium-3, which results in few or no neutrons. Figure 4 shows the uses of helium in 2002.

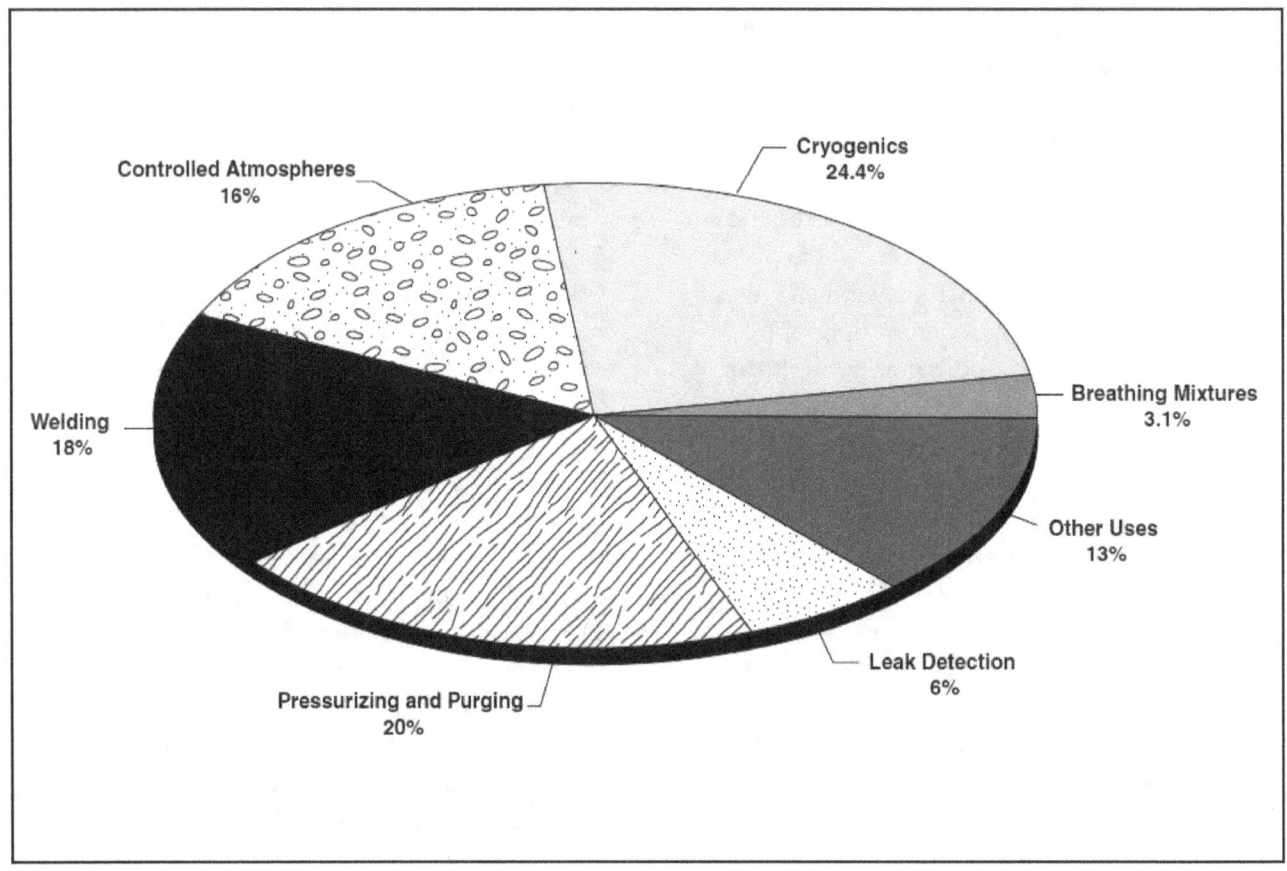

Figure 4. Uses of helium in 2002.

Current Helium Business

Historical production and extraction of helium in the United States is shown in Figure 5. The figure indicates a steady growth in helium recovered and sold since 1971, with greater percentage increases from 1986 to 1988, and smaller growth from 1988 to 1992. Domestic helium sales were affected by the Algerian helium plant coming online around 1994. This is where the figure shows a decline in sales. Growth increased dramatically in late 1986 when Exxon Corporation began extraction of helium from Riley Ridge Field, Wyoming, at their Shute Creek plant. The extraction capability of this plant was recently increased from approximately 1.2 Bcf to 1.4 Bcf of pure helium per year, with the addition of a helium liquifier. Most of the growth in helium recovery since 1986 has been from the mid-continent area extraction plants. These plants sold about 900 MMcf of helium in 1987; in 2002, they sold about 3,106 MMcf of helium, which computes to an average annual growth of approximately 8.6 percent.

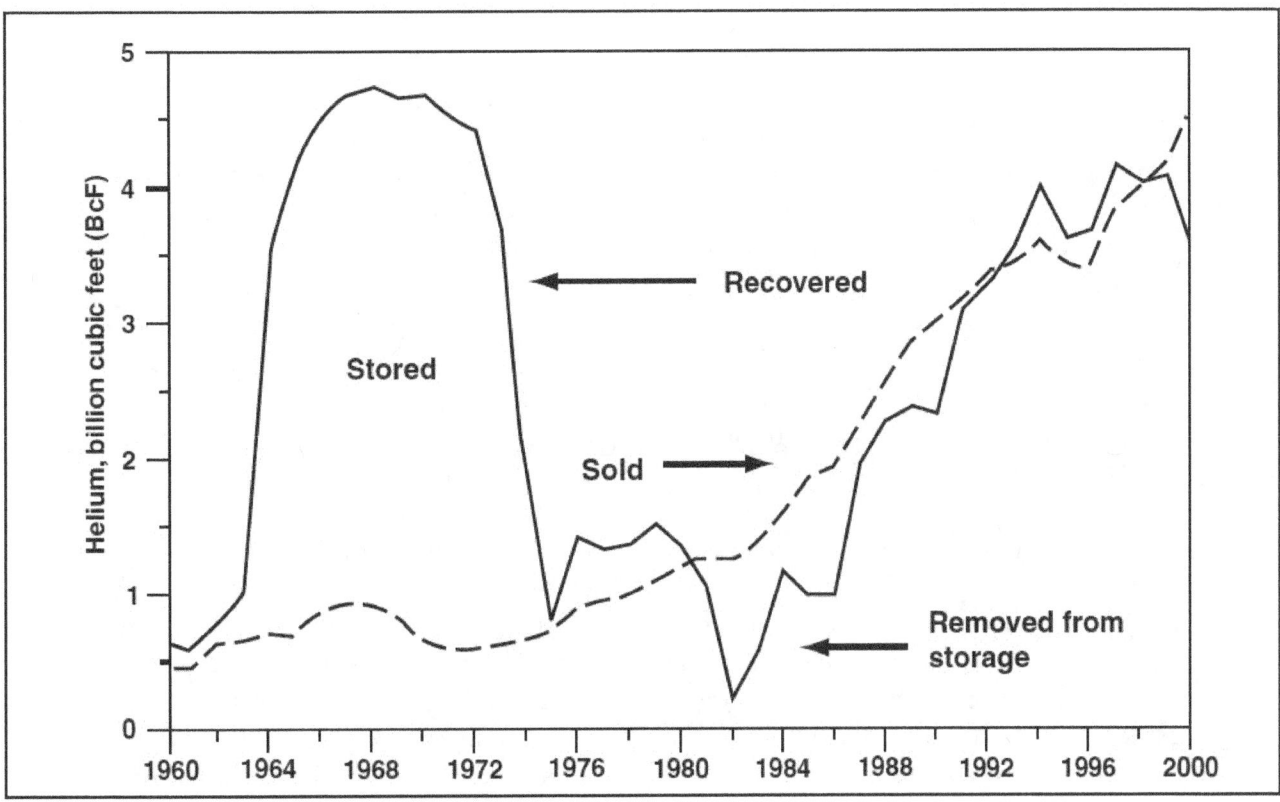

Figure 5. Historical production and extraction of helium in the United States.

Figure 6 shows the projected production and sales of helium from the mid-continent area through the year 2015. The area between the sales and production lines is the estimated withdrawal from Cliffside Storage to meet demand. Riley Ridge area helium production and extraction was not included in this projection because helium extraction at the Shute Creek plant is near capacity, excluding any additional plant changes, which would allow for greater plant gas throughput.

The helium recovery curve is based on the projected decline of gas from the helium-rich natural gasfields in Kansas, Oklahoma, and Texas. These fields include Bradshaw,

Greenwood, Kansas Hugoton, and Panoma Fields in Kansas; Guymon-Hugoton and Keyes in Oklahoma; and West Panhandle and Texas Hugoton in Texas. The possible decline of helium sales through technological advances or production of helium outside the United States may play a major role in the future of the helium industry. The sales of United States produced helium in 2002 decreased approximately 4 percent compared to 2001 sales (16).

Presently, it is estimated that the extraction of helium from natural gas in the mid-continent area is from 75 to 80 percent of the total annual available helium. This represents the helium recovered at the crude helium plants. A portion of the gathered natural gas is used to run compression with the helium contained in that natural gas lost to the atmosphere. Also, some helium is lost at the crude helium and pure helium plants. These losses are estimated to be 10 to 15 percent, excluding any possible gathering system losses. The addition of compression will burn more natural gas and thus losses of helium will increase, if the gathered natural gas continues to be used as fuel for compression.

Crude helium plants in the mid-continent have an extraction capacity of about 3 Bcf per year. However, only about 1.7 Bcf of this capacity was utilized during 2002. One crude helium plant continues to run intermittently, and had no production for about three-quarters of 2002. Private industry withdrew a net amount of 1,408 MMcf of helium from the Cliffside Gasfield during 2002. The net withdrawal of helium started again in 1999 when about 113 MMcf of helium was produced from Cliffside.

Pure Helium

- There are pure helium extraction plants in Qatar and Algeria that will provide additional helium production of about 900 MMcf per year, which is less than the rated design capacity of the two helium plants. During the preparation of this report, an explosion occurred that destroyed three of the six liquefied natural gas (LNG) processing units at the Skikda plant in Algeria. The helium extraction is expected to come online in 2005, but will be at about 300 MMcf per year of the 600 MMcf per year rated helium plant capacity. The three LNG processing units are expected to be replaced allowing extraction of about 600 MMcf per year, but the time for completion of this project is not known. The extraction at Qatar is expected to begin during the fourth quarter of 2005. The helium extraction at the Algeria and Qatar plants should reach approximately 1.2 Bcf per year, at some point in the future.

- A project continues to be discussed for Apache County, Arizona. The helium would be produced from a high carbon dioxide gas stream. The carbon dioxide is being considered for tertiary recovery of oil, per new releases issued by the lease holder. The Permian Basin and California have been discussed as possible locations for use of the carbon dioxide. If the project is undertaken, it has been stated that a helium plant capable of producing about 600 MMcf per year would be built. This is considered to be a long-term project, with no date being projected for completion.

- A helium extraction plant started operations near Shiprock, New Mexico, in 2002. This is a smaller scale plant, but the exact extraction capability is not known. This plant was moved from Chillicothe, Texas, where helium extraction ceased during 2002.

- A small helium plant began extraction near Dodge City, Kansas, during 2002. The design capacity of the plant is not known, but the plant is producing very little helium.

- The BLM is aware of three additional helium extraction projects being considered in the United States. Details of the projects are not known, and confidentiality does not allow disclosure of the locations being considered for the production of helium.

Crude Helium

- A crude helium plant located along the conservation pipeline is not operating at capacity. This plant was not operating approximately three-quarters of the year during 2002.

- The Baker plant ceased crude helium production during 2002. This gas is being processed at another plant with crude helium extraction capabilities.

- A plant capable of producing crude helium was built in Ness County, Kansas, with a design capacity of 5 MMcf per day of gas. The helium content of the gas was reported as being 1.6 percent and coming from the Ryersee Field. The helium will be upgraded to 90 plus percent for shipping and delivered in gaseous form to a pure helium plant for further processing. It has been reported that gas processing has started, but that has not been confirmed by the BLM.

Explanation of Figure 6 Graph

The graph presented in this report has been changed to depict the estimated helium that may be taken from the Cliffside Gasfield to meet helium demand. Cliffside is expected to be in withdrawal mode for the immediate future, and it is likely that this trend will continue. The graph represents a simplistic view of the actual pure helium sales that are to be expected. The actual pure helium sales and crude helium extraction will not follow a straight line, but will be a jagged curve. This is based on several factors that include, but are not limited to, pure helium sale declines or increases, plant problems, and additional pure helium extraction. The production of crude helium from the Cliffside Gasfield is impacted by any of the above, or any event that causes changes in the helium market. The estimated versus actual data will fluctuate on a year-to-year basis. For instance, the helium estimated (on the graph) to be withdrawn from the Cliffside Gasfield during 2002 was about 1,315 MMcf, but actual demand was 1,408 MMcf.

The actual mid-continent helium sales data has been used for 1999 through 2002. The helium sold in the mid-continent in 2003 and 2004 is estimated to be similar to 2002 sales. Thereafter, growth is assumed to be 200 MMcf per year. The Algerian and Qatar plants are assumed to be operational toward the end of 2005, with 300 MMcf per year of helium produced during 2005. The production is assumed to be 900 MMcf per year in 2006. These plants should reach a helium extraction capability of 1.2 Bcf. This depends to a great extent on the decision to rebuild the LNG facilities at the Skikda plant in Algeria, and the time needed to accomplish this task. This will bring the helium extraction capabilities to approximately 1.2 Bcf. The additional 300 MMcf per year to bring the total helium extraction to 600 MMcf per year from the Skikda plant is not shown on the graph.

The private pure helium plants connected to the Cliffside Gasfield via the Government's conservation pipeline have a combined nameplate capacity of about 4 BCF. However, it is thought that the actual helium extraction capability is closer to 3.8 BCF, excluding any additional capacity being added in the future. The pure helium plants' capacity is depicted by the solid line on the graph (Figure 6).

The crude-helium recovery depicted on the graph is the estimated annual helium to be extracted from natural gas in the mid-continent area. The crude-helium extracted as a percentage of helium available was escalated from the current 75 to 80 percent to 90 percent over the time period covered. This would mean that all helium would be extracted, except the losses at the compressors and the plants. The rate of decline of the available helium that can be recovered from natural gas in the mid-continent is set at 10 percent per year over the time period. This decline appears to reflect the helium available for extraction reasonably well at this time. This does not account for crude-helium plants being down or other helium production problems outside the mid-continent area. The rate of decline of production in the mid-continent area may be greater than 10 percent in the future.

The total production of helium from the Cliffside Gasfield is set at 2.3 Bcf per year. This is in accordance with the straight-line sales method used to offer the helium for sale as called for in the Helium Privatization Act of 1996. The 2.3 Bcf includes open market sales of 2.1 Bcf and approximately 0.2 Bcf of in-kind helium sales. The indication would be that 2003 and 2004 would be the only years in which 2.3 Bcf would boost production to private pure helium plant capacity along the conservation pipeline. The pure helium plant capacity was not utilized during 2003, and it is not expected that pure helium plant capacity will be reached during 2004. The years following would indicate that pure total helium plant capacity along the pipeline will not be utilized, and additional amounts of helium outside Cliffside Gasfield will need to be exploited to meet helium demand.

The 2.3 Bcf withdrawal rate sets the upper limit for withdrawal of helium from the Cliffside Gasfield. Since the last report, open market sales of Government-owned helium have been instituted to make helium available for purchase by private industry. The Government sold 2.3 Bcf of the 4.2 Bcf of helium offered during the two open market sales.

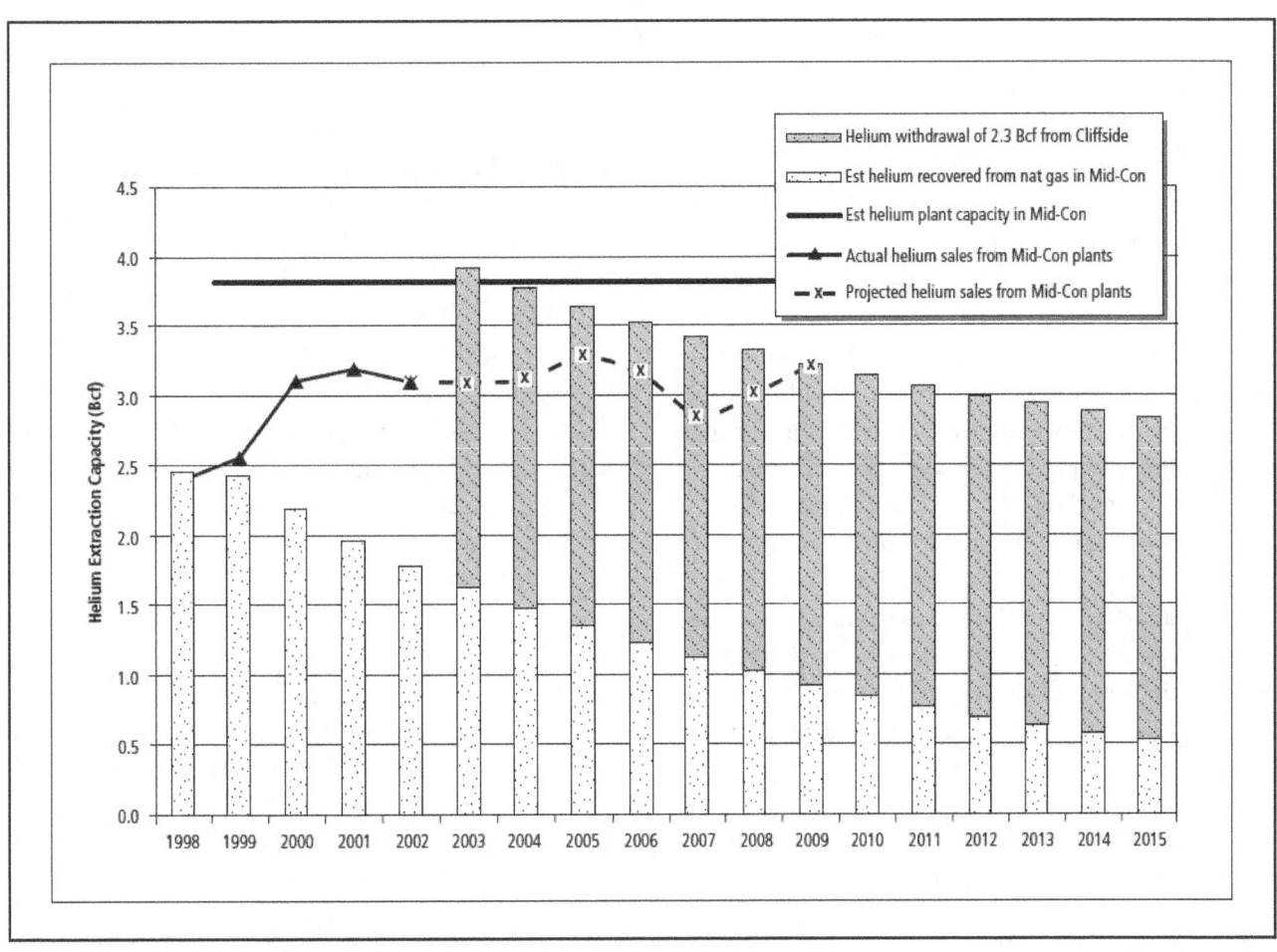

Figure 6. The impact of sales and declining crude helium extraction in the mid-continent area on the cliffside Gasfield.

Summary

This report uses several criteria to determine reserves, marginal reserves, and subeconomic resources, including helium content, proximity to major gas transmission lines, and size of field. In previous reports, it was concluded that relatively large volumes of helium would be available from natural gas through 2020, although that helium would probably be in gases with leaner concentrations than those being processed today. This report does not estimate nationwide projections for helium in natural gas production. Rather, the report focuses on short-term supply and demand for helium and examines the possible need for additional helium, with focus on the Cliffside Gasfield. The Figure 6 graph is used to project the possible need for helium to be delivered from Cliffside Gasfield, and to show the need for additional helium extraction. The Cliffside Gasfield plays a vital role in helping to supply worldwide helium demand. The near term source of helium is the Government's helium supply being sold on the open market. The Qatar and Algeria projects are expected to begin helium production during 2005. The helium extraction at the Algerian Skikda plant will initially be about 300 MMcf per year and should reach 600 MMcf per year, at some point in the future. The helium demand on Cliffside Gasfield should be diminished by the additional helium production, but it is not expected to eliminate helium production from the Cliffside Gasfield.

As of December 31, 2002, there are 30.8 Bcf of helium stored in Bush Dome at Cliffside Gasfield. The Government owns 29.2 Bcf and 1.6 Bcf is owned by private companies. There are also approximately 3.7 Bcf of helium contained in the natural gas in Bush Dome. The present trend is withdrawal of helium from Cliffside Gasfield to meet demand. The open market sale of the Government's helium has been started in compliance with the Helium Privatization Act of 1996. The Government offered 2.1 Bcf of helium for sale in March and again in October of 2003 with 1.64 Bcf and 0.68 Bcf sold, respectively. Future open market sales will be held to correspond with the Government's fiscal year, which begins in October.

There are nondepleting fields throughout the United States that contain helium resources; however, several factors will need to be considered prior to production of this gas. Some of the factors are: 1) the location of the field(s), 2) the helium resources of the field(s), 3) the economics of helium extraction from the natural gas stream of the field(s), and 4) field(s) located on Federal lands may be restricted by regulations from processing the gas stream for the sole purpose of helium extraction. Revised helium regulations are being developed and will be published for comments in the Federal Register during 2004.

Sales have remained basically flat since 2000 and the outlook for helium sales is not certain. Considering the estimated sales growth, helium production from Algeria and Qatar, and helium available for extraction from natural gas in the mid-continent area (Figure 6), it would appear that Cliffside Gasfield will meet excess helium demand until about 2009. At that point, additional helium production will be needed to meet demand.

References

1. Moore, B.J. 1976. Helium Resources of the United States, 1973. BuMines IC8708. 17 pp.

2. ___. 1979. Helium Resources of the United States, 1977. BuMines IC8803. 25 pp.

3. ___. 1979. Helium Resources of the United States, 1979. BuMines IC8831. 27 pp.

4. Hertweck, F.R., Jr. and R.D. Miller. 1983. Helium Resources of the United States, 1981. BuMines IC8927. 17 pp.

5. Miller, R.D. 1985. Helium Resources of the United States, 1983. BuMines IC9028. 17 pp.

6. ___. 1987. Helium Resources of the United States, 1985. BuMines IC9130. 16 pp.

7. ___. 1988. Helium Resources of the United States, 1987. BuMines IC9189. 17 pp.

8. Miller, R.D. and John E. Hamak. 1990. Helium Resources of the United States, 1989. BuMines IC9267. 14 pp.

9. Hamak, J.E. and B.D. Gage. 1993. Helium Resources of the United States, 1991. BuMines IC9342. 18 pp.

10. Hamak, J.E. and D.L. Driskill. 1995. Helium Resources of the United States, 1993. BuMines IC9436. 18 pp.

11. Gage, B.D. and D.L. Driskill. 1998. Helium Resources of the United States, 1997, Technical Note 403. Bureau of Land Management. BLM/HE/ST-98/002+3700. 28 pp.

12. ___. 2001. Helium Resources of the United States, 2001, Technical Note 408. Bureau of Land Management. BLM/HE/ST-98/002+3700. 30 pp.

13. Potential Gas Committee. 2001. Potential Supply of Natural Gas in the United States (as of December 31, 2000). Potential Gas Agency, Colorado Sch. Mines, Golden, Colorado. 346 pp.

14. Department of Energy, Energy Information Administration. 2000. US Crude Oil, Natural Gas, and Natural Gas Liquids Reserves. 1996 Annual Report. DOE/EIA-0216(99). 156 pp.

15. Tongish, Claude A. 1980. Helium – Its Relationship to Geologic Systems and its Occurrence with the Natural Gases, Nitrogen, Carbon Dioxide, and Argon. BuMines R18444. 176 pp.

16. Pacheco, Norbert. 2003. Helium. 2002 Annual Report. United States Geological Survey, Reston,Virginia. 11 pp.

Bibliography

Anderson, C.C. and H.H. Hinson. 1951. Helium-Bearing Natural Gases of the United States, Analyses and Analytical Methods. BuMines 486. 141 pp.

Boone, W.J., Jr. 1958. Helium-Bearing Natural Gases of the United States, Analyses and Analytical Methods. Supplement to Bulletin 486. BuMines 576. 117 pp.

Bureau of Land Management, Helium Operations. 1998. Analyses of Natural Gases, 1917-95. CD-ROM. NTIS PB 97-502611.

Cardwell, L.E. and L.F. Benton. 1970. Analyses of Natural Gases of the United States, 1968. BuMines IC8443. 169 pp.

___. 1970. Analyses of Natural Gases, 1969. Bu Mines IC8475. 1970, 134 pp.

___. 1971. Analyses of Natural Gases, 1970. BuMines IC8518. 130 pp.

___. 1972. Analyses of Natural Gases, 1971. BuMines IC8554. 163 pp.

___. 1973. Analyses of Natural Gases, 1972. BuMines IC8607. 104 pp.

Gage, B.D. and D.L. Driskill. 1998. Analyses of Natural Gases, 1996-97, Technical Note 404. Bureau of Land Management. BLM/HE/ST-98/003+3700. 71 pp.

___. 2003. Analyses of Natural Gases, 1998-2001, Technical Note 412. Bureau of Land Management. BLM/NM/ST-03/001+3700. 173 pp.

Hamak, J.E. and S. Sigler. 1989. Analyses of Natural Gases, 1988. BuMines IC9225. 66 pp.

___. 1990. Analyses of Natural Gases, 1989. BuMines IC9256. 61 pp.

___. 1991. Analyses of Natural Gases, 1990. BuMines IC9290. 56 pp.

___. 1991. Analyses of Natural Gases, 1986-90. BuMines IC9301. 315 pp.

Hamak, J.E. and B.D. Gage. 1992. Analyses of Natural Gases, 1991. BuMines IC9318. 97 pp.

Hamak, J.E. and S. Sigler. 1993. Analyses of Natural Gases, 1992. BuMines IC9356. 62 pp.

Hamak, J.E. and D.L. Driskill. 1996. Analyses of Natural Gases, 1994-95, Technical Note 399. Bureau of Land Management. BLM/HE/ST-97/002+3700. 68 pp.

Hertweck, F.R., Jr. and R.D. Miller. 1983. Helium Resources of the United States, 1981. BuMines IC8927. 17 pp.

Hertweck, F.R., Jr. and D.D. Fox. 1984. Analyses of Natural Gases, 1983. BuMines IC8993. 127 pp.

Miller, R.D. and G.P. Norrell. 1964. Analyses of Natural Gases of the United States, 1961. BuMines IC8221. 148 pp.

___. 1964. Analyses of Natural Gases of the United States, 1962. BuMines IC8239. 120 pp.

___. 1965. Analyses of Natural Gases of the United States, 1963. BuMines IC8241. 102 pp.

Miller, R.D. 1985. Helium Resources of the United States, 1983. BuMines IC9028. 17 pp.

Miller, R.D. and F.R. Hertweck, Jr. Analyses of Natural Gases, 1981. BuMines IC8890, 1982, 84 pp.

___. 1983. Analyses of Natural Gases. 1982. BuMines IC8942. 100 pp.

Moore, B.J. 1974. Analyses of Natural Gases, 1973. BuMines IC8658. 96 pp.

___. 1975. Analyses of Natural Gases, 1974. BuMines IC8684. 122 pp.

___. 1976. Analyses of Natural Gases, 1917-74. BuMines Computer Printout. NTIS PB 251 202/AS. 889 pp.

___. 1976. Helium Resources of the United States, 1973. BuMines IC8708. 17 pp.

___. 1976. Analyses of Natural Gases, 1975. BuMines IC8717. 82 pp.

___. 1977. Analyses of Natural Gases, 1976. BuMines IC8749. 94 pp.

___. 1978. Analyses of Natural Gases, 1977. BuMines IC8780. 95 pp.

___. 1979. Analyses of Natural Gases, 1978. BuMines IC8810. 113 pp.

___. 1979. Helium Resources of the United States, 1977. BuMines IC8803. 25 pp.

___. 1980. Analyses of Natural Gases, 1979. BuMines IC8833. 100 pp.

___. 1980. Helium Resources of the United States, 1979. BuMines IC8831. 27 pp.

___. 1981. Analyses of Natural Gases, 1980. BuMines IC8856. 236 pp.

___. 1982. Analyses of Natural Gases, 1917-80. BuMines IC8870. 1,055 pp.

Moore, B.J. and J.E. Hamak. 1985. Analyses of Natural Gases, 1984. BuMines IC9046. 102 pp.

Moore, B.J., R.D. Miller, and R.D. Shrewsbury. 1996. Analyses of Natural Gases of the United States, 1964. BuMines IC8302. 144 pp.

___. 1966. Analyses of Natural Gases of the United States, 1965. BuMines IC8316. 181 pp.

___. 1967. Analyses of Natural Gases, 1966. BuMines IC8356. 130 pp.

___. 1968. Analyses of Natural Gases of the United States, 1967. BuMines IC8395. 187 pp.

Moore, B.J. and S. Sigler. 1985. Analyses of Natural Gases, 1985. BuMines IC9096. 182 pp.

___. 1987. Analyses of Natural Gases, 1917-85. BuMines IC9129. 1,197 pp.

___. 1987. Analyses of Natural Gases, 1986. BuMines IC9167. 101 pp.

___. 1988. Analyses of Natural Gases, 1987. BuMines IC9188. 74 pp.

Munnerlyn, R.D. and R.D. Miller. 1963. Helium-Bearing Natural Gases of the United States: Analyses. Second Supplement to Bulletin 486. BuMines 617. 93 pp.

Sigler, S.M. 1994. Analyses of Natural Gases, 1993. BuMines IC9400. 58 pp.

Glossary of Reserve and Resource Terms

The following definitions are based on definitions found in *Principles of a Resource/Reserve Classification of Minerals, Geological Survey Circular 831, 1980*, with additions and revisions where necessary to accommodate for helium.

Demonstrated – A term for the sum of measured and indicated.

Identified Resources – Resources whose location, grade, quality, and quantity are known or estimated from specific geologic evidence. Identified Resources include reserves, marginal reserves, and subeconomic resources components. To reflect varying degrees of geologic certainty, these economic divisions can be subdivided into measured, indicated, and inferred.[5]

Indicated – Quantity and quality are computed from information similar to that used for measured resources, but the amounts are less certain and can be estimated with a degree of certainty sufficient to indicate they are more likely to be recovered than not. In general, they include reserves in formations that appear to be productive based on log characteristics but that lack core data or definitive tests, and reserves that will be found by field extensions, in-fill drilling, or improved recovery methods.

Inferred – Estimates are based on an assumed continuity beyond measured and/or indicated resources, for which there is geologic evidence. Inferred resources may or may not be supported by analyses or measurements.

Inferred Reserve Base – The in-place part of an identified resource from which inferred reserves, marginal reserves, and subeconomic resources are estimated. Quantitative estimates are based largely on knowledge of the geologic character of a reservoir and for which there may be no gas analyses or measurements.

Marginal Reserves – That part of the reserve base which, at the time of determination, borders on being economically producible. Its essential characteristic is economic uncertainty. Included are resources that would be producible, given postulated changes in economic or technologic factors.

---

[5] The terms *proved*, *probable*, and *possible*, which are commonly used by industry in economic evaluations of ore or mineral fuels in specific deposits, reservoirs, or districts, have been loosely interchanged with the terms *measured*, *indicated*, and *inferred*. The former terms are not a part of this classification system.

Measured – The quantity is computed from dimensions revealed by actual gas analyses; production or formation tests, electric logs, and core analyses; and/or delineated by drilling and defined by fluid contacts or undrilled areas that can be reasonably judged as commercially productive on the basis of geologic and engineering data.

Other Occurrences – Resources that are contained in extremely low helium content natural gases or nonconventional natural gas reserves. Only "proved" and "probable" natural gas reserves of this type are evaluated and included in the classification.

Reserves – That part of the reserve base that is economically extracted or produced at the time of determination. The term "reserves," as used in this report, is for fields from which helium is being extracted from the gas stream. Reserves include only recoverable materials; thus, terms such as "extractable reserves" and "recoverable reserves" are redundant and are not a part of this classification system.

Reserve Base – That part of an identified resource that meets specified minimum physical and chemical criteria related to current drilling and production practices, including those for quality, porosity, permeability, thickness, and depth. The reserve base is the in-place demonstrated resource from which reserves are estimated. It may encompass those parts of the resources that have a reasonable potential for becoming economically available within planning horizons beyond those that assume proven technology and current economics. The reserve base includes those resources that are currently considered reserves, marginal reserves, and some of those considered subeconomic resources. For helium, the measured portion of subeconomic resources is included in the reserve base but not in the indicated portion.

Resource – A concentration of naturally occurring solid, liquid, or gaseous material in or on the earth's crust in such form and amount that economic extraction of a commodity from the concentration is currently or potentially feasible.

Subeconomic Resources – The part of identified resources that does not meet the economic criteria of reserves and marginal reserves.

Undiscovered Resources – Resources, the existence of which are only postulated, comprising deposits that are separate from identified resources. The undiscovered resources of helium are postulated based on the "speculative" resources reported by the Potential Gas Committee (PGC).

APPENDIX A
Guidelines for Determining Helium
Reserves and Resources

The following guidelines apply for determining helium reserves, marginal helium reserves, and subeconomic helium resources as contained in this publication. The guidelines also are helpful for determining undiscovered resources.

Individual Field Reserves and Resources

Helium Content %	Contained Helium in Field/Area	Category
		Reserves*
>=0.30	150 MMcf - 1 Bcf	Marginal Reserves
>=0.30	10 - 150 MMcf	Subeconomic Resources
0.10 - 0.30	1 - 5 Bcf	Subeconomic Resources
0.10 - 0.30	150 MMcf - 1 Bcf	Subeconomic Resources
0.10 - 0.30	10 - 150MMcf	Other Occurrences
0.05 - 0.10	>=5 Bcf	Subeconomic Resources
0.05 - 0.10	10 MMcf - 5 Bcf	Other Occurrences
<0.05	Large coalbed methane or carbon dioxide resources, >5 Bcf contained helium	Other Occurrences

The previous guidelines also apply for areawide classifications. In addition, the following guidelines are applied to basinwide resources. An average helium content is used for each basin and the reserves/resources determined by applying the average helium content to the basin's gas resource estimate for probable and possible categories. For the undiscovered resources, the average helium content is applied to minimum, most likely, and maximum speculative PGC gas resource numbers.

Areawide Classifications

< 0.05	All DOE/EIA reserves after subtracting computerized database measured reserves	Other Occurrences
<0.05	PGC probable gas resources in a basin or region.	Other Occurrences
ALL	PGC possible gas resources in a basin or region.	Subeconomic ** Resources

* Extraction is taking place from the fields and formations that are being produced. Therefore, there is no need for a designation based on helium content of the natural gas.

** The move from Marginal Reserves to Subeconomic Resources was made based on the determination that extraction of helium from these sources is not likely.

www.ingramcontent.com/pod-product-compliance
Lightning Source LLC
Chambersburg PA
CBHW052022280526
45793CB00005B/1080